# BEING I

: This is a quick read summary based on the book
"Being Mortal"
by Atul Gawande

# NOTE TO READERS:

This is a Summary & Analysis of Being Mortal, by Atul Gawande. You are encouraged to buy the full version.

# Table of Contents

# OVERVIEW

This review of *Being Mortal: Medicine and What Matters in the End* by Atul Gawande provides a chapter by chapter detailed summary followed by an analysis and critique of the strengths and weaknesses of this book.

Gawande draws on clinical studies, case histories and stories from his own experiences as a doctor and a son to illuminate the subject of mortality relative to modern medical systems. His treatment of the subject covers a broad range of institutions and individuals that shape the lives of the aged and terminally ill. The central thesis of the book is that the experience of the end of life has been problematized and addressed by medical models that place extending life over quality of life and institutional frameworks that place safety and efficiency over the ability for people to have autonomy over the last part of their lives.

Gawande is a surgeon at Brigham and Women's Hospital and a professor at the Harvard Medical School. He is a writer at *The New Yorker* magazine and author of three *New York Times* bestselling books.

# SUMMARY

## Introduction

Gawande explains that tending to the needs of the dying and their loved ones seemed beside the point in medical school. Confronting mortality was simply outside the jurisdiction of what was taught. Instead, students were taught to diagnose and cure or treat disease, and to understand all the complex mechanisms of the body to repair injuries. It was not until he began to practice that he realized how unprepared he was for the realities of the dying. He had no training to deal with mortality.

As a junior surgical resident Gawande had a patient named Joseph Lazaroff who was suffering badly from an incurable cancer. After radiation failed to shrink the tumor, the only option left was surgery. Doctors were aware that even with surgery the cancer could not be cured, and that at best treatment would extend his life by a few months of bed ridden misery. The surgery was high risk in terms of even surviving the procedure, and post-surgical complications were projected to be severe. The doctors gave Lazaroff the option, and he chose the surgical treatment which was by all accounts a success in terms what could be expected. However, complications from it overwhelmed Lazaroff and he died two weeks later when his son approved his removal from life support.

Gawande, reflecting on the story of Lazaroff, argues there was a fundamental failure in this case for doctors to really come to terms with the full reality of this man's mortality and their own limitations. The heroic efforts to save him were doomed before they began and the doctors were aware of this fact, but unable to fully confront it, or effectively communicate this to the patient. In addition, real guidance in the face of the realities of this situation were not within the repertoire of the oncologists, surgeons, and other specialists involved in his care. The training needed to provide comfort and sympathy, in the face of this man's certain death, was simply absent. His argument here is not that individual doctors were to blame for this, rather that modern medical systems more broadly speaking simply lack the preparation for the realities of death.

As recently as the mid-forties most people died in their homes and as early as the eighties less than 20 percent did. Nothing in medical school really prepared Gawande for death, and his first experiences with it as a doctor haunted him. During his training the focus was on beating the malady and once in practice Gawande was suddenly confronted with the fact that medicine does not always win. The problem, he argues, is not when there is a remedy, treatment or surgery that can save someone, but when there is not. It is this moment for which modern medicine has no answers for adequately dealing with the reality of mortality. Gawande argues that only by taking an honest and frank accounting of the realities of death and the experiences of dying can we make rational and ethical choices about how well health systems are serving this population. This book is an examination of those realities.

# Chapter 1: The Independent Self

In this chapter the author explores the theme of independence, including how it is defined, what it means to people, and how medical institutions have become a location in our culture for dealing with the problem of loss of independence. In America there are standards for determining the level of independence a person has. There are eight "Activities of Daily Living" that include being able to: walk, get out of a chair, get out of bed, use the bathroom, eat, dress, bathe and groom. If a person is unable to accomplish these things on their own they are said to lack physical independence. There are also eight "Independent Activities of Daily Living" that include being able to: shop, prepare food, housekeep, do laundry, take medications, make phone calls, travel and manage finances. If a person lacks the ability to do these tasks without assistance the medical community would consider them unable to safely live independently.

Gawande shares a story about his grandfather who lived to be 110 years old. Although he could only perform some of the activities required for basic independence in the context of Western medicine, after a lifetime of farming and raising his children, family systems in India made sure that he could continue to live at home and live as he pleased. Younger generations in India, although this is changing, simply make sure that elders are taken care of and receive the support they need as they lose some of the functionality required for daily living. In America the same kinds of family systems have been in place until the modern era. For the bulk of human history, the aged or sick have been cared for by family members in multigenerational family systems.

Becoming aged used to be a rare occurrence and elders were perceived to have special wisdom and authority as a result. For example, prior to the 1800's people would often misrepresent their age as older, in contrast to today where people are more likely to make efforts to be perceived as younger. He argues that some of this diminished authority is because surviving to older ages is much less rare today, and also that technology and communication have diminished the role that elders once had for being the holders of special wisdom. In addition, because younger people used to be able to expect to inherit their parents' wealth earlier in their lives, there was an economic incentive built in to family systems to make sacrifices in order to care for aging parents. Modern economies offer more opportunities for economic independence separate from family systems, and family systems have changed in tandem with that.

The author argues that these changes have not been all negative. Emerging economic realities include retirement systems and the independent economic security of children. These have both given older people the benefits of independence and freedom from the dependence of intergenerational family systems. Longer lifespans and new economic realities have changed modern family systems and retirement communities offer an example of how a focus on extending independence into older ages has been embraced. There remains the inevitability, however, that independence is bound to eventually become impossible. Aging is not a process that generally ends with independence.

# Chapter 2: Things Fall Apart

In this chapter the author examines what happens when independence is lost, specifically from advancing age. He also investigates how well the medical profession is equipped to deal with the realities of aging given that modern medicine is built around the concept of fixing disease and injury, and ultimately the onset of age is not something medicine can arrest. He also looks at the role that geriatric specialists can play both in the lives of aging patients, and in terms of training general practitioners perspectives on the special needs and priorities of older patients.

Gawande describes that modern medicine has not only prolonged life, but also changed what he calls the trajectory of life. Prior to modern medicine generally life and health were stable until a disease or injury ended life over the course of minutes to months. However, the treatment options available today create different shapes of trajectories. In the case of chronic and progressive disease the trajectory has dips and rebounds but maintains a decline over time. In the more typical case there are declines followed with plateaus amounting to a more gradual decline than in previous historical periods. The course of our lives, therefore, has been altered by medicine in profound ways, as has our cultural understanding of the process of aging.

There are competing theories as to what causes aging. Despite some evidence that suggests a genetic link to aging, Gawande argues that there is much more evidence to suggest that aging is, in fact, a general wear and tear process whereby the systems in the body slowly breakdown. As is typical of complex systems with lots of redundancy built in, the breakdown is gradual and across all body systems.

Culturally the demographics of humans have shifted away from a pyramid shape with the young representing the largest portion at the bottom in terms of their representation of the population, to a more rectangular spread where the aged are closer to equally represented in the population. Gawande argues we have not culturally come to terms with this shift in demography. In terms of medical practice, for example, specialists in geriatrics and adult primary care have actually decreased in the last twenty years while proportionally the population of older people has grown. Part of this decline is the fact that these specialties command smaller salaries, and part of it is a distaste for working with the elderly. There is no glory in treating the ailments of the elderly since there is no fix for aging, no surgery or medication to stop the aging process.

There are some that do choose these specialties and the author spends some time recounting a story from a visit he had in a geriatrician's practice. During the patient visit the geriatrician asked the patient about her daily life and routines and took note of details such as how the patient got up from the chair and how she was walking. With an awareness of the quality of life issues at this age, and the most common debilitating issues for people of this age, such as falling and breaking a hip, the doctor paid special attention to her feet even though the patient did not mention they were bothering her. But after a close examination he realized they needed treatment and referred her to a podiatrist.

Most of medicine is very good at diagnosing and fixing a single isolated problem. But as the system of our complex bodies breaks down gradually, the problems can not all be fixed. However, that does not mean they cannot be addressed. Gawande cites research done at the University of Minnesota. Half of the 568 people over the age of seventy who lived independently but had chronic health problems were assigned to see a group of geriatric nurses and doctors, the others saw only their regular doctors. After a year and a half the same percentage in each group had died, but the group that had seen the geriatric specialists were 25% less likely to have become disabled and 50% fewer developed depression. The also had a 40% lower rate of needing in home healthcare services. Much of the work the team did was to simplify medications and make sure that patients were eating well, maintaining social connections, and had good foot health and safe homes.

However, Medicare does not cover geriatric services and this and other economic pressures has resulted in the closing of many geriatric centers at hospitals across the country. Gawande argues that this is in part due to the kind of attention that technology, such as pace makers, and pharmaceuticals get rather than the rather dull mundane things that geriatrics are trained to ask questions about: diet, social habits and feet. Geriatricians ultimately cannot make the kinds of promises that we want our modern medicine to deliver. They cannot solve the problem that they are engaging daily, that is, decline and ultimately death. The author maintains, however, that their contributions in extending independence and quality of life to the aged are significant and undervalued.

It may be too late to train enough geriatric specialists to cover the needs of the growing aging population because it takes so much time to train them. However, another solution offered by the author could be to add geriatric training to that of primary care doctors and nurses. Right now 97% of medical students have no training in geriatrics.

# Chapter 3: Dependence

In this chapter the author looks at nursing homes. He uses historical evidence and case studies to demonstrate that nursing homes have their roots in medical ways of thinking and suggests that such paradigms may not best represent the needs or desires of older people. A primary argument he makes is that safety and efficiency have become the dominant lens through which residents become patients and severe restrictions on liberty as a result leave many residents of nursing homes feel more like prisoners than people free to make decisions about their own lives.

Eventually, disability will likely rob many of the aged of their ability to live independently. More than half of Americans will spend at least one year in an assisted living facility. The author highlights this with a story about an aging couple. The progression of disability, even when there is a loving and willing partner to manage care, can become simply too exhausting and unsustainable. He then details the story of his grandmother-in-law as she adjusted to nursing home living after several incidents at home made safety a serious concern. Although the facility had a strong community, many regularly scheduled activities and as well as organized trips, Alice was not adjusting well. Having experienced a high degree of independence before the move to the senior living facility, she found the institutional rules, regulations and regimens to be oppressive. Faced with the loss of her sense of freedom, she fell into depression.

At this point the author examines some history. Prior to Social Security the only option many older people had once the inevitable disabilities of aging left them with no opportunities to earn money were poorhouses or almshouses unless they had family that could take them in. Poorhouses in the early 1900's housed those incapacitated by debilitating mental illness or alcoholism alongside the aged and were essentially places of incarceration. Conditions were terrible and included infestations of vermin, bedbugs, flies and fostered spread of contagious disease such as tuberculosis. During the Great Depression growing numbers of people forced into these conditions sparked national attention and Social Security was passed in 1935. This allowed more Americans to continue to support themselves independent of institutions. On an international level, poorhouses continue to be a solution for the aged in many industrializing nations, and Gawande details some examples from India.

Gawande argues that the transition from the poorhouse model to the modern day nursing home model was framed by an understanding of the problem as a medical one. In the late 1930's there was a shift towards putting the disabled aged in hospitals at a time when the primary function of hospitals was focused on custodial care. By World War II, largely a result of the rise of antibiotics and blood pressure medications, the priorities of the hospital shifted towards temporary stays for the purpose of treating then discharging people. This period was followed by a massive growth spurt in the construction of hospitals, which fundamentally shifted the cultural experience of sickness from the home to these institutions. By the 1950's the elderly who would enter hospitals and not regain enough independence to be discharged, were straining that system. By 1954 legislation was passed to fund custodial units that were separate, and yet still medically centered, facilities. This was the context for the birth of the modern nursing home.

In contrast to the poorhouses of the early twentieth century, modern retirement communities are a vast improvement in terms of many dimensions of care including sanitation, health care standards, activities to help provide a sense of community, and proper nutrition. However, argues Gawande, they are still lacking in important ways. Returning to the case of Alice, his grandmother-in-law, the author details more specifically the ways in which the regimens of daily routine were experienced as a deep loss of independence such as constant supervision, being forced to use a walker for safety reasons, and enforced compliance with medication protocols. For Alice, the loss of her home and sense of independence was very depressing. As her disabilities increased with age she transitioned to higher levels of care in the ladder system of care intensity and with each move up that ladder she lost more freedom and endured a deeper sense of loss of control. Her feeling was that she was imprisoned.

The problem that the author is pointing to here is that the institutional manifestation of caring was in conflict with Alice's idea of a meaningful life. He further suggests this is a pattern arguing that resistance to institutional regimes is common and is a phenomenon that nurses have worked out specific strategies for engaging. Rather than creating space to try to see resistance as an indication that needs are not being met and seeking solutions based on those circumstances, there is great institutional pressure to always work towards compliance with established protocols based in medical perspectives of safety, liability and institutional efficiency.

# Chapter 4: Assistance

There is a tendency to see what we have as a system and think that it is better than any alternative but Gawande argues that we should have a bigger imagination based on awareness of the current problems to continue to improve this important part of our lives. In this chapter he uses several case studies of individuals and institutions to further demonstrate both the challenges and success stories of dealing with the loss of independence. Again the author focuses on the tendency of current systems to put safety and efficiency concerns about the rights and desires of people to control their own lives.

One of the personal stories that the author uses is in this chapter is that of Shelley and her father Lou Sanders. After a series of falls and other progressive health issues it became clear that Lou was not able to live independently and Shelley made arrangements for him to come to live with her and her family. Shelley who was already raising children and working took on his care responsibilities and managed the best that she could, however over time his health issues, and the logistical challenges that come with them became more than she could juggle. This additional labor included helping him adjust to the new living arrangements, helping him find new social connections, managing medications, preparing special food, hospital trips for increasingly frequent falls. As his aging progressed and is abilities decreased she became responsible for basic bodily needs as well such as bathing and changing diapers. Tensions to be a good daughter with being a good mother, wife and employee reached a breaking point. They eventually settled on looking for assisted living, the middle ground solution between home and a nursing home.

At this point in the story Gawande turns to Karen Brown Wilson. In the 1980s, when faced with her own mother's unhappy experience in a nursing home, Wilson began to conceive of assisted living as a place that could be a solution to the problems that her aging mother was facing in a nursing home. The original concept was meant as an alternative, not a transitional place, to the nursing home. Wilson got her PhD in gerontology after working in senior services for years. She was able to see the various dimensions of senior care from multiple perspectives including not only those of residents but also staff and administrators. She saw safety as the predominant justification for institutional control and tried to shift focus more onto giving residents as much autonomy as possible. After struggling to make with change in existing institutions, she and her husband oversaw construction of a new facility.

In this new apartment complex the focus was on tenants who had control over their own lives but access to care and help if they needed it. For example, they scheduled time with nurses instead of the institution forcing them to conform to a schedule. The nurses entered the tenant's home, which affected the power dynamics of those relationships. They had call buttons for emergencies but were not subject to the daily controls of medical staff. They could eat what and when they wanted and entertain guests as they saw fit. Critics saw the design as dangerous and Wilson tried to incorporate the concerns from the critique into the model without fundamentally sacrificing the privacy and freedom at the core of the project. Collecting and tracking data on cognitive functioning, happiness of residents, and basic health metrics allowed the program to demonstrate that it was a success along all of these lines, and in particular, that the cost was lower than nursing homes.

The idea was a success and clearly had a market. Their company went public and the concept spread to other states rapidly. However the rapid uptake of the idea included the cooptation of the term assisted living and once the idea was out of Wilson's hands, the original concept got lost or watered down. What ended up in practice was that the facilities were reframed as a middle of the way solution towards a nursing home eventuality, driven in large part by profit motives. The idea of "continuum of care" became a way to understand assisted living as part of a system that ended in nursing home care. Further, concern about litigation and safety of the medical aspects of this care started to once again dominate the policy choices at these places to be that of safety over autonomy.

# Chapter 5: A Better Life

In this chapter the author explores a few alternative models to nursing homes and offers some reflection on what has made these models so successful, as well as a glimpse into the lives of those who envisioned and fought for them.

In 1991 Bill Thomas, a few years after becoming a medical doctor, became medical director at Chase Memorial Nursing Home. The facility was home to eighty disabled elderly people. He was not happy with how things were at the nursing home and found the patients to be depressed about the situation as well. Influenced in part by his own farm living, his plan to change the home for the better included bringing in life to the nursing home in the form of plants, dogs, cats, and birds. His experiment met with significant difficulties in terms of funding and logistical problems, but eventually his vision came to fruition. Positive changes happened as a result. Residents got involved in taking responsibility for the care of the animals. Gawande argues that this renewed a sense of purpose for many. It also put the nurses and the residents in a position where they had to solve problems by working together, destabilizing some of the entrenched power dynamics of those relationships. Overall, residents started showing noticeable improvement, and although there was some resistance from staff to the nature of their added responsibilities, there was willingness to solve those problems because it was clearly helping residents feel more aware, alert and engaged. Both physical and psychological improvements were being noted by the staff.

Chase Memorial also became the site of a study and over the course of two years empirical data was collected to assess the new program by comparing it to another nearby nursing home. A number of positive indicators were noted such as significantly lower use of prescriptions and a 15% lower death rate. The author also uses several anecdotal stories to demonstrate the turnaround in the individual lives of residents. He largely credits these changes with being given more life purpose and suggests that even though this is hard to empirically measure, is a very important dimension of people's lives. He further argues that as people age, things like ambition to achieve great things or accumulate wealth has a natural decline and priorities shift towards more modest aims focused on connecting to the world in their immediate surroundings.

The next example the author turns us to is the NewBridge on the Charles retirement community in Boston. One example of the way this home was built to encourage a sense of community and foster a big family like atmosphere was the open floor plan architecture and pod style arrangement with small groups of people sharing daily life in the common spaces. The staff focused on giving residents as much latitude and choice as they could, even if that sometimes meant that there was some tension between safety and the desires of the elderly person. Although without animals as a central theme like Chase Memorial, there were children from a nearby school that shared yard space and in several cases the residents would volunteer as tutors or librarians. The author also details some of the challenges that director Jacquie Carson had to face, particularly in terms of a medical community that continually seemed to demand more control over the daily lives of residents in the form of enforced protocols and restrictions of freedoms.

The author returns to a central theme as he describes these alternative institutions and the people that work and live there. The lives of the disabled elderly are not best understood or valued through the framework of a medical and institutional lens of safety and efficiency as the only priorities. Providing environments that foster a sense of purpose and as much autonomy as possible create opportunities for not just more full filling quality of life for residents, but better health outcomes.

# Chapter 6: Letting Go

In this chapter Gawande explores the end of life through a series of vignettes including stories from the lives of patients, hospice and palliative care providers, oncologists and even his own experiences as a doctor. The fundamental critique that he makes in this chapter is that the perspectives of the medical community are often at odds with the real needs and desires of patients and the inability of modern medicine to really come to terms with mortality in ways that capture important elements of the process of dying for many people. In particular, at what point do medical interventions cease to make sense, and how can medical professionals become better equipped to offer patients more guidance and support in making difficult decisions about dying.

At 34 and pregnant, Sara Thomas Monopoli was diagnosed with lung cancer. Oncologists wanted to start treatment immediately and delivery was induced at 39 weeks. At first there were some hopeful treatment options, but as the best options proved unhelpful, secondary and tertiary treatment options with less and less chances of being successful were tried. Meanwhile, her quality of life continued to deteriorate and what little energy she had was spent enduring treatments and the suffering of their side effects. As treatment progressed, doctors originally somewhat hopeful for significant prolonged life expectancy began suggesting treatments with marginal success rates and at best offered weeks or months of time. He follows her progression through four rounds of chemotherapy and shows the way at every turn doctors, patients and family were not prepared to fully confront the reality that she was dying.

The author shows that survival rates always have a thin long tail when we plot their distribution. There are always outliers, people that survive despite seemingly impossible odds. He argues that doctors, despite recognizing the near impossible odds, feel pressure to focus on optimism in the face of patients' hopes and fears. He argues that doctors have not been properly equipped for the task of helping patients and family members make these decisions. Patients and families then often take on the battle mode ethos of a medical establishment designed around fixing and curing, and engage in the battle without a clear sense of their options or consideration of their own desires. Studies suggest that people do not place short term survival gains above things such as not having to suffer, connecting with family and friends, and the basic comfort of being in their own homes.

Gawande follows Sarah Creed, a hospice nurse, on her rounds, giving the reader perspective into the very different concerns of palliative care than that of surgeons and oncologists. The priorities of care in this context are shifted towards providing for comfort from both pain and side effects of treatments, prolonging consciousness, working with family, and making sure basic needs are being met. The priorities for hospice care is not to do nothing at all, but rather shift priorities from extending life at every cost to making life right now as full as possible for those with limited time left. Through hospice care, people are offered the potential for a different kind of death, not in a sterile place surrounded by machines and strangers, but at home in peaceful surroundings.

Despite the potential benefits of hospice care, it lives in tension with a story about fighting. People want to see themselves as fighters, and fighters want to fight until there is nothing more that doctors can do. The problem is that there is very rarely a time where there is nothing that doctors can do, right up until the very end. This very often means a progression of interventions right up until death. Gawande argues that it is not even a choice in many cases, it is a default reaction created in part by an almost mystical belief in the ability of modern medicine to perform miracles in the face of impossible odds. Often times options such as hospice or palliative care are not discussed as potential avenues because doctors specialized in oncology are not trained to have conversations about such matters.

The author then turns to several studies concerning the choices that people make when given access to other options earlier in the treatment process. Aetna insurance company, for example, found that offering more extensive coverage of palliative care significantly decreased patients' visits to ICUs despite not lowering coverage for such interventions. A study from Massachusetts General Hospital in 2010 showed that patients offered palliative care in conjunction with oncology care stopped treatments sooner, had less suffering, and lived 25% longer. This, argues Gawande, is evidence that not only are some of our medical interventions creating suffering at the last stage of life, their primary justification, the extension of life, may actually be reduced. Finally, an initiative led by medical leaders in LaCrosse Wisconsin made discussing end-of-life wishes a part of routine for those entering hospitals or nursing homes, the percentage of such advance directives jumped from 15 to 85 percent.

# Chapter 7: Hard Conversations

Gawande tells the story of his own father's experience with a cancer affecting his spinal chord with a special focus on decision points along his journey as the primary means to explore the dimensions of enabling patient centered decisions in the treatment of terminal illness. He emphasizes the importance of the different roles that doctor and family can play, and sheds light on an important goal, that is, providing ways for patients to be the authors of their own life.

To provide some context for his narrative, the author discusses global demographic trends relative to economic development. In the first of three stages, the model most associated with high levels of poverty and underdevelopment, most people die at home without much access to medical systems. As countries develop, more facilities and middle class people shifts the trend towards higher levels of intervention and significantly more deaths occur in institutional environments. Finally, in the third stage, much like in the U.S. now, the experience of death moves back to the home. Gawande suggests that this last transition is occurring in the U.S. but that although there is a resistance to the institutionalized version of death, new systems for death in the home have not been fully established as the norm. However, hospice and palliative care seems to be the primary way in which this transition is taking place.

The author then investigates three kinds of doctor patient relationships. First is the paternalistic kind of relationship in which the doctor largely makes decisions about treatment based on expertise alone followed by telling the patient what the treatment will be. This model has been largely replaced in medical training for a few decades. The informative style, when doctors establish treatment options and explain the associated risks and benefits to patients and allow them to decide among the options, is likely the most common kind of doctor patient interaction in U.S. medical contexts today. Gawande notes that although this is an improvement in terms of empowering patients, it still sets priorities in medical terms, that is, prolonging life is the main benefit described in terminal cases. A third style called shared decision making, however, starts with doctors getting a sense of the patients own priorities before discussing treatment options. The doctor in this sense shifts the evaluation of treatment options to be in line with patient objectives, be they about prolonging life, comfort at the end of life, or preserving energy for spending with family and friends.

At various points in the story about his father and his progressive journey with cancer it is this final strategy that is the most successful in terms of giving his father the power to be the author of his own life, a metaphor Gawande returns to often as ideal. For example, when the original diagnosis came Gawande and his father, who is also a surgeon, met with two specialists to discuss options. The first fluctuated between the first two models, paternalistic and informative. This doctor was adamant that radical and immediate surgery was really the only course of action to take because paralysis was an inevitable outcome of the progression of the disease. A second doctor used the shared decision making style and quickly established the priorities of Gawande's father, and together they crafted a plan that involved closely monitoring the progression of the tumor and being realistic about the fact that the surgery carried a very high risk of immediate paralysis. In the end they decided for the second treatment option. It turned out that it would be two and a half years later before his symptoms worsened enough to have to reopen decisions about treatment and in the meantime he was able to continue to live a full and active life.

When his father's condition started to worsen, Gawande struggled to have hard conversations with him about his wishes for the next stage of his life. Despite the difficulty of the conversations, there was a sense of clarity afterwards as priorities were made clear. He decided to have the surgery and armed with information on the priorities of his father, Gawande was able to make sound decisions during the surgery when the surgeon made him aware of complications at a critical turning point created by complications during the operation. However, after surgery was successful more decisions had to be made concerning further treatments such as chemotherapy. Gawande shares his own sense of failing at this juncture when lured by the optimism of the oncologists, he pressed his father to undergo such treatments. After months of suffering the severe side effects of treatment and rapid deterioration of his abilities to enjoy even modest life priorities, the tumor did not shrink as predicted.

At this point another consultation with an informative style oncologist happened and several potential additional treatment options were put on the table. The author clearly shows in this interaction that the priorities of his father, to have as much time and quality of life to spend with friends and family, were being overshadowed by treatment options couched in terms of prolonging life no matter the cost. It was time to consider other options, and Gawande had hard conversations with his parents to look at other potentials such as nursing homes or hospice. Ultimately his father was very receptive to considering hospice, even though the idea was quite horrifying to his mother. It meant facing the reality of his mortality.

Ultimately Gawande's father chose hospice care. The author describes how the hospice nurse's priorities were clearly in line with what his father wanted most. In addition, he describes that there was a gradual and steady improvement that he suggests is a direct result of the palliative care that his father received. He is careful here to also highlight the special expertise that these nurses had which enabled quality of life to be both goal and outcome of their treatment efforts. The palliative care had given Gawande's father room to live.

# Chapter 8: Courage

In the final chapter of the book, Gawande explores the topic of courage and shares with the reader the last weeks of his father's death experience as well as returning to one of his own cases opened in a previous chapter. He argues that there are two kinds of courage relevant to death. First is the courage to face mortality and its realities, including its fears and hopes. The second is to act on that awareness. In fact, for the dying as well as their doctors and family, such decisions are, in the end, exceedingly difficult even with the best clarity on the options available.

The author argues that risk assessment alone is simply too thin a paradigm to fully capture the definition of problem of dying because it ignores in large part both the tremendous cost of suffering and the value of intangibles such as being conscious enough to share last moments with family. He summarizes research by Daniel Kahneman that looked at how nearly 300 patients experienced pain as they underwent kidney stone and colonoscopy procedures fully awake. Kahneman developed a model he called the Peak-end rule. This rule described what was consistent from the experimental results: people's experience of pain in the moment, and their memories of pain are vastly different. Further, memories of pain tend to focus on two moments: the peak part of the pain and the final moments of the procedure. In other words, patients asked to recall pain would settle on something closer to the average between the peak pain of the procedure and the moments at the end. Duration of pain seemed to not be significant in this memory.

This suggests a gulf between the remembering self, and the experiencing self, which then begs the question of if they are in conflict, how can we decide between them? In particular, what does it mean for doctors trying to help patients make decisions about treatment in the decision sharing model most preferred by Gawande? Although Gawande does not offer much in the way of a practical solutions for this formulation of the problem, he does illustrate what some of the complications are in coming to terms with what patient's priorities are. It becomes another level of awareness that doctors can use in assisting decision making about treatment options.

A final issue that Gawande explores in this treatise on mortality and modern medical systems is that of assisted suicide. It is clear that Gawande is ambivalent on this issue. However, he makes a strong case that in medical contexts were assisted suicide is a clear option, and palliative care is not also a clear option, many patients may choose suicide without realizing there is an option besides progressively invasive and aggressive treatments. Patients need to know there are palliative care options that may yet still provide them with time left of life worth living.

Returning to his father's experience of death Gawande recalls in agonizing detail the difficult decisions and excruciating moments of his father's last weeks. For example, despite his father's clear wishes to the contrary, his mother called emergency services instead of hospice when one day he was unable to be roused from a medicated fog. His father was angry upon waking in the hospital. Gawande does not dismiss the pain of his mother who was just not ready to let go of her husband and instead demonstrates how the decisions of caretakers are themselves full of contradictions and overwhelming emotions. Even with forethought, discussion and planning decisions surrounding dying are still fraught with ambiguity and unease.

# Epilogue

In the epilogue the author reviews the main arguments of the book and highlights the take away lessons. Modern medicine is too narrowly focused on survival, and in the case of the dying, this means medical systems are missing important aspects of patient's lives such as quality of life, and the ability to extend a life worth living as opposed to extending life at any cost. Palliative care, he argues, offers some solution to these oversights, however, as long as it remains completely separate from the rest of the medical establishment and decision making processes, it does not have the full impact that it could. Medical professionals in general, argues Gawande, need to be thinking more in terms of allowing patient goals and desires enter into treatment decision making.

# ANALYSIS

Atul Gawande brings sensitivity, experience, expertise and wisdom to the subject of dying in his book *Being Mortal: Medicine and What Matters in the End*. The work is a masterful dovetailing of personal stories and anecdotes with research and case histories that successfully communicates the institutional and personal complexities of grappling with mortality. The argument that our current systems have failed to fully take into consideration the experience of the dying is compelling and well supported.

Gawande is strongest at crafting narratives around specific case histories and detailing his personal experiences, both as a doctor and as a son of a dying man. He brings in enough context to make the people in his stories come to life. There are many passages where the author gives insight into his own emergent awareness of the problems in institutions and practices of which he himself is a participant. These moments of self-reflection do not come off as contrived but rather as entirely genuine turning points in his own thinking about these issues. Not only do such moments offer insight into the momentum of existing practices and methodologies, they offer a profound opportunity to visualize change as possible. In addition, by highlighting the contributions of mavericks such as Bill Thomas and Karen Brown Wilson, he shows that resistance to traditional practices can and does have the potential to create meaningful change.

Gawande does tend to open more questions than he is prepared to fully answer. Much of his solutions are more theoretical and suggestive. There is a rather concrete framing of the problem, but an abstract set of solutions. There are places in the book where certain solutions seem to be clear, such as including geriatric training in medical school for general practitioners, and increasing awareness of palliative care options earlier in the process of considering treatment choices. However, overall the reader is left wanting for more such practical solutions. It may be best to situate this work as one that is starting a much needed conversation on a topic that people are reluctant to discuss, and as such, perhaps asking questions is more important than answering them.

Another weakness of the book is that it focuses much more on physical disability with the advancement of age than it does on mental deterioration. There is simply not enough treatment of issues surrounding the difficult decisions institutions and families have to make in cases where the ability for the dying to make sound decisions becomes unclear. What does it mean, for instance, to talk about the ability for people to author their own lives when their ability to come to terms with reality is severely compromised? What does it mean to put autonomy before safety in such cases? This is a rather large oversight on the part of the author and it may belie his reticence to tackle this difficult ethical terrain, or perhaps it is simply a matter of his own occupational bias as a surgeon rather than a psychiatric professional. Either way, this important issue is barely discussed in the book and it does present some significant challenges to the idea that allowing people to be the author of their own lives could and should be the center of a new paradigm for designing programs and institutions for those in advanced stages of dying.

Likewise, a more thorough treatment of costs would have been appropriate. Rising healthcare costs are a serious concern in economically advanced economies. While this is discussed in reference to a few of the specific programs he investigates, Gawande fails to provide enough information on managing costs to address the critique that efficiency in institutional settings plays a critical role in keeping healthcare costs manageable in the 21st century. Surely institutional efficiency is also an important aspect of designing care for the elderly and terminally ill and yet this subject does not get sufficient treatment in this book. Likewise, legal issues and liability issues, sometimes waived off by the author as if they are trivial profit driven concerns, are serious road blocks to putting autonomy before safety. These questions will certainly need to be addressed in order for a major shift to occur concerning policies and institutions of the kind the author is hopeful for.

This book has several key audiences that would benefit greatly from considering the perspectives of the author and the research that he has assembled in this work. First and foremost, medical professionals of all varieties would likely find this book provocative and worth the read, particularly those who come into contact on a regular basis with the aged or terminally ill. Second, as difficult as it may be, those with family members and friends who are struggling with advanced age or terminal illnesses would likely benefit from an opportunity to consider the ideas in this book. They would be in a better position to fully help loved ones to articulate their own priorities for treatment or assisted living arrangements. Finally, because all people will eventually grapple with these issues, the book is relevant to a broad audience. It is few among us who will evade having to confront the kinds of issues this author has raised and, as such, this book will have a wide impact.

44372042R00027

Made in the USA
San Bernardino, CA
13 January 2017